THE FROME HOARD

SAM MOORHEAD, ANNA BOOTH AND ROGER BLAND

THE BRITISH MUSEUM PRESS

Sam Moorhead, Anna Booth and Roger Bland have asserted
the right to be identified as the authors of this work

First published in 2010 by The British Museum Press
A division of The British Museum Company Ltd
38 Russell Square
London WC1B 3QQ

www.britishmuseum.org

A catalogue record for this book is available from the British Library

ISBN: 978-0-7141-2334-9

The papers used in this book are recyclable products and the manufacturing processes
are expected to conform to the environmental regulations of the country of origin.

Designed by Zoë Mellors
Printed in Frome, Somerset, with the generous support of Butler Tanner & Dennis

50p from the sale of every book will go to the Frome Hoard appeal fund. Your donation will support the
efforts by Somerset County Council to acquire the hoard and commission the necessary conservation and
research. In the event that the attempt to acquire the hoard is unsuccessful, your donation will be used to
support a related programme of research, conservation, interpretation and education.

CONTENTS

ACKNOWLEDGEMENTS

The way in which the hoard was discovered and excavated and the work that has been done so far to conserve and study it has been an excellent example of co-operation between many different individuals and organizations. We would like to thank them for their contributions to the project.

We start with Dave Crisp, who found the hoard, for reporting it so promptly and, above all, for leaving it in the ground, so allowing it to be excavated archaeologically. Geoff and Anne Sheppard, the owners of the land where the find was made, have also been extremely co-operative.

Katie Hinds, Finds Liaison Officer for Wiltshire, played an essential role in setting the wheels in motion for the excavation and was involved throughout, while Bob Croft and Naomi Payne of Somerset County Council Heritage Service very quickly commissioned the excavation, which was masterfully led by Alan Graham. We are also grateful to GSB Prospection of Bradford for carrying out a geophysical survey. Steve Minnitt of Somerset County Council Heritage Service has also been exceedingly helpful, as have Simon Clifford and Elizabeth Kulh of Somerset County Council Communications Team, and Lawrence Bostock of Somerset County Council Heritage Service who took the images of the siliquae. Andrew Mackay of Tullie House Museum, Carlisle kindly supplied an image of the milestone of Carausius at very short notice.

At the British Museum Pippa Pearce did a remarkable job in leading the initial washing of all the coins with help from Jamie Hood, Anna Tang, Ellen Van Bork and Janina Parol. Dan Pett built an extensive web resource at www.finds.org.uk/fromehoard at very short notice.

We are also grateful to other colleagues in the British Museum for their help: Richard Abdy, Benjamin Alsop, Olivia Buck, Stephen Dodd, Sherry Doyle, Henry

Flynn, Eleanor Ghey, Megan Gooch, Thomas Hockenhull, Richard Hobbs, Janet Larkin, Ian Leins, Claudio Mari, Owain Morris, Nicholas Newbery, Ian Richardson, Olivia Rickman, David Saunders and Esme Wilson. This book was only made possible by the rapid action of Rosemary Bradley, Naomi Waters, Lily de Gatacre and Axelle Russo at the British Museum Press, with excellent design work by Zöe Mellors.

   We were fortunate to work with John Hayes Fisher and Gemma Hagen of 360 Productions on filming the hoard for the BBC television series Digging for Britain.

   We are very grateful to Victor Ambrus for generously donating a wonderful reconstruction artwork at very short notice.

   The production of this book could not have been realized without the generosity of Butler Tanner & Dennis in Frome.

Sam Moorhead, Anna Booth and Roger Bland

NOTE ON THE TEXT

The coin denominations mentioned in the book are as follows:

Denarius (pl. denarii): the standard Roman silver coin made regularly from 211 BC to AD 240, when it was replaced by the radiate.

Aureus (pl. aurei): the principal gold coin of the early Roman Empire.

Radiate (pl. radiates): a name commonly given to a coin first produced in AD 215, which shows the emperor wearing the Sun God's crown of rays. The earliest coins were silver but they quickly became debased.

Siliqua (pl. siliquae): a coin of high-quality silver first made by Constantine I (306–37)

I | DISCOVERY AND EXCAVATION

The first indication that the field where the Frome Hoard was found was going to be particularly interesting came on 9 April 2010, when Dave Crisp discovered a scattering of fourth-century Roman silver siliquae (coins of high-quality silver) (see chapter VII) with his metal detector. Dave has been a keen metal-detector user since 1988 and has already reported more than 300 finds to his local Finds Liaison Officer for the Portable Antiquities Scheme in Wiltshire, Katie Hinds.

1.1 Above: **Alan Graham** excavating the Frome Hoard

Dave was searching on this field, which at the time was under pasture but which had formerly been ploughed, with the permission of the landowner. On 11 April 2010, two days after he discovered the siliquae, Dave returned to the site. He began to work his way into the field and about 100 m away from the area where the silver coins were found he received an unusual signal. Upon digging a small hole to investigate further he realized that he had hit the top of a pottery vessel containing some bronze coins. Recognizing that he might be dealing with a hoard, he dug no further, filled the hole back in and decided to report his find immediately so that it could be excavated by archaeologists.

Straight away Dave contacted Katie Hinds who quickly realized that the site was just over the border into Somerset and called the Finds Liaison Officer for that county, Anna Booth. With the help of her colleagues in the Somerset Heritage Service, Naomi Payne (Historic Environment Officer) and Robert Croft (County Archaeologist), Anna arranged for local archaeologist, Alan Graham, to lead an excavation of the site. Over the course of three days Alan, with the help of Katie, Anna, Dave, the landowner's family and others, excavated the hoard in its entirety (figs 1.1, 1.2).

Once the topsoil had been removed the outline of the original pit became visible, as a mottled darker oval area against the brown natural clay. Initially there had been little indication of the size of the hoard. Dave had retrieved a few small earthenware sherds when he discovered it and at first these appeared to belong to the base of a fairly small vessel. However, it now

became clear they in fact formed part of a small upturned dish, which had been used as a lid for a much larger pot. As the shoulders of the vessel appeared, it was revealed that this was a greyware storage jar, which was cracked but complete (60 cm tall and 45 cm in diameter) (fig. 1.3). One sherd had slipped slightly, allowing a glimpse of the interior, which was filled with bronze coins. It also appeared that the sides of the pot had been carefully packed with some sort of plant material by those who had buried it.

At this point a decision had to be made about whether the hoard should be removed *en bloc* or excavated in parts. Due

1.5 Above: The bottom of the pot with a few coins left

to the sheer size and weight of the hoard, it was decided that it would be impossible with the available resources to remove it in one piece; furthermore, the pot was already broken into several pieces so it would not have been possible to keep the coins in their original positions. The pot was therefore carefully dismantled from the top down and the coins were removed in numbered layers (figs 1.3, 1.4, 1.5, 1.6). It was

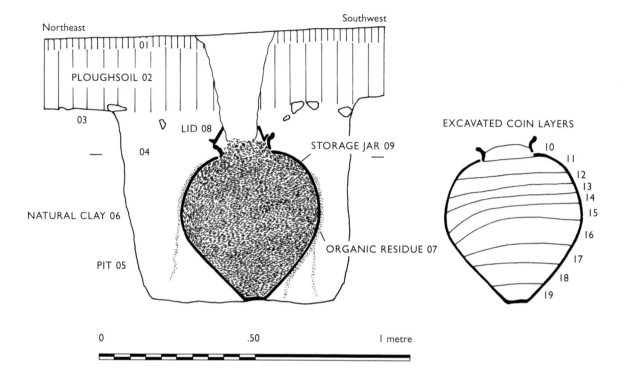

Northeast

Southwest

01

PLOUGHSOIL 02

03

LID 08

04

STORAGE JAR 09

NATURAL CLAY 06

ORGANIC RESIDUE 07

PIT 05

EXCAVATED COIN LAYERS

10
11
12
13
14
15
16
17
18
19

0   .50   I metre

hoped that this method would provide additional information about the distribution of the coins during the analysis process. The coins from each layer were immediately placed into labelled bags and packed into boxes to protect them and prevent them from drying out. In total more than sixty bags of coins were collected over the course of three days. The excavation had been a tremendous success, enabling us to speculate with much more confidence about the circumstances surrounding the burial of the hoard.

1.6. Above: Section drawing of the excavation by Alan Graham, showing how the pot was excavated in layers

CONSERVATION AND STUDY

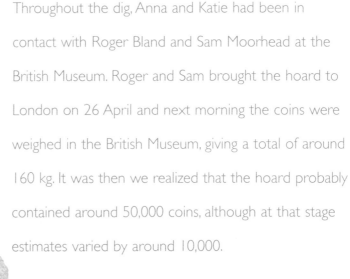

Throughout the dig, Anna and Katie had been in contact with Roger Bland and Sam Moorhead at the British Museum. Roger and Sam brought the hoard to London on 26 April and next morning the coins were weighed in the British Museum, giving a total of around 160 kg. It was then we realized that the hoard probably contained around 50,000 coins, although at that stage estimates varied by around 10,000.

A more immediate observation was that much of the hoard had been waterlogged in the ground. Not only did this add a little to the weight but it also meant that there was a serious conservation issue. Roger and Sam quickly organized a meeting with David Saunders (Head of Conservation and Science at the British Museum) and Pippa Pearce (Metals Conservator) who agreed that the coins should be washed and dried before they dried out naturally. Had they been left to dry, many of the oxides would have solidified, making later conservation work much more complicated and expensive. In the space of about eight weeks, Pippa and her colleagues washed and dried the entire hoard – a major achievement.

As the coins were washed, Roger and Sam, with assistance from other colleagues, started to sort the coins by emperor. This took ten weeks: it enabled us to gain an overview of the contents of the hoard and provided basic information needed for the Coroner's Report.

2.1 Above: A group of washed coins ready for sorting

CHAPTER

III | CIRCUMSTANCES OF BURIAL

We are very fortunate that Dave Crisp's promptness in reporting his discovery has meant that we have much more information than is normal for a Roman coin hoard. Because of the ways in which most coin hoards have been found and recovered, it is rare to have any clues as to why they were buried. The excavation revealed how the pot was carefully nestled in the ground, apparently with packing material (fig. 1.6). A dish was placed over the top as a lid and then it seems the hoard was not disturbed again.

Because of the sheer number and weight of the coins, it seems highly unlikely that the pot was filled with coins before being buried; it would have been extremely difficult to manhandle and would probably have broken before it could have been placed in the ground. The pot was broken into about forty pieces when discovered. It is just possible that the pot did contain coins before it was buried and that it was broken when placed in the ground. However, had this been the case it would surely not have maintained its shape. More likely, the pot was broken after burial, possibly due to later settling of the earth and expansion of the contents as a result of waterlogging. It is even possible that the movement of tractors above caused the damage. If the pot was placed in the ground before filling, we can imagine many smaller pots or bags of coins being tipped into it. This is supported by the large group of Carausian coins found in Layer 16 – one such smaller pot of coins appears to have mainly consisted of his pieces. This underlines the importance of careful excavation as it provides an insight into the way the pot was filled. Given that the latest coins appear to be of Carausius (286–93), a breakaway Roman emperor, it is possible that the hoard is connected with the political upheavals that probably accompanied his assassination in AD 293.

3.1 Below: Dave Crisp visits the British Museum during the sorting of the coins

CHAPTER

IV | CONTENT OF THE HOARD

The coins range in date from AD 253 to 293, covering a period of about forty years and were struck at mints across the Empire (fig. 4.2). For much of this period, in addition to the core 'Central Empire', there were breakaway dominions. Between AD 260 and 274 a succession of seven rulers held power over Gaul and Britain, the so-called 'Gallic Empire', while between AD 286 and 296 Carausius and Allectus ruled over Britain and part of Gaul.

4.1. Above: **Copper alloy radiate of Postumus (260–9), probably struck at Trier (Frome Hoard) (17 mm)**

London
Cologne
Trier
GALLIC EMPIRE
Lyons
Ticinum • Milan
Siscia
Rome
CENTRAL EMPIRE
Cyzicus
Antioch

There are very few higher quality silver radiates from the reigns of Valerian (253–60) and Postumus (260–9) (fig. 4.1); either these coins had left circulation by the time the hoard was buried, or they were deliberately excluded. The majority of the coins are base silver radiates (with less than five per cent silver) struck by Gallienus (260–8) (fig. 4.3), and his wife Salonina (fig. 4.4), Claudius II (268–70) and the Gallic emperors Victorinus (269–71) (fig. 4.5) and the Tetrici (271–4) (fig 4.6). These are among

4.3 Above and left: Copper alloy radiate of Gallienus (260–8) struck at Rome showing Pegasus (Frome Hoard) (19 mm)

17

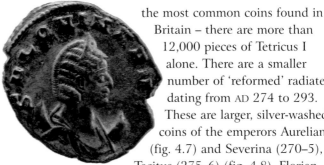

4.4 Above and right: Copper alloy radiate of Salonina (260–8) struck at Milan (Frome Hoard) (17 mm)

the most common coins found in Britain – there are more than 12,000 pieces of Tetricus I alone. There are a smaller number of 'reformed' radiates dating from AD 274 to 293. These are larger, silver-washed coins of the emperors Aurelian (fig. 4.7) and Severina (270–5), Tacitus (275–6) (fig. 4.8), Florian (276) (fig. 4.9), Probus (276–82) (fig. 4.10), the family of Carus (282–4) (figs 4.11, 4.12), Diocletian (284–305) and Maximian (286–305) (fig. 4.13).

Very exciting is the concentration of coins of the British emperor Carausius (286–93) found in Layer 16 (just over halfway down the pot) (fig. 1.6). So far 766 of his coins have been identified, but once all the illegible coins have been cleaned this number will rise and we expect that there will be more than 800 of his coins in the hoard, making this the largest group of his coins ever found in Britain. Most surprising, however, is that among the Carausian

4.5 Above and right: Copper alloy radiate of Victorinus (269–71), probably struck at Trier (Frome Hoard) (19 mm)

4.6 Above and right Copper alloy radiate of Tetricus I (271–4), probably struck at Cologne (Frome Hoard) (18 mm)

coins are five silver denarii – these are rare coins not normally found in hoards. Furthermore, they are in perfect condition – the best examples we have ever seen, suggesting that they had barely been in general circulation at the time of burial (figs 5.4, 5.5, 5.10, 5.12).

At present the coins of Carausius are the latest in the hoard, although it is just possible that there is a later coin among the 11,212 that still need to be conserved before they can be identified. At present, no coins of his henchman (then assassin), Allectus (293–6) have been identified. So, on present evidence, it would seem that the hoard was buried around AD 293, a very precise date.

Determining the exact number of coins in the hoard is easier said than done! There are several lumps of corroded coins, in some cases coins are fused together, and there are a number of fragments. At present the total we have is 52,503.

4.7 Left and above: Silver-washed radiate of Aurelian (270–5), struck at Rome (Frome Hoard) (22 mm)

4.8 Left and above: Silver-washed radiate of Tacitus (275–6), struck at Siscia (Croatia) (Frome Hoard) (23 mm)

4.9 Left and above: Silver-washed radiate of Florian (276), struck at Lyons (Frome Hoard) (23 mm)

4.10 Above and left: Silver-washed radiate of Probus (276–82), struck at Ticinum (Pavia) (Frome Hoard) (24 mm)

4.11 Above and right: Silver-washed commemorative radiate of Carus (282–3), struck at Rome (Frome Hoard) (22 mm)

Central Empire	Dates	Total
Valerian and Gallienus *(joint reign)*	253–60	46
Gallienus *(sole reign)*	260–8	6,091
Salonina *(wife of Gallienus)*	260–8	404
Claudius II	268–70	5,421
Divus Claudius	270–1	1,227
Quintillus	270	333
Aurelian	270–5	266
Severina *(wife of Aurelian)*	270–5	13
Tacitus	275–6	252
Florian	276	10
Probus	276–82	619
Carus	282–3	8
Divus Carus	283	5
Magnia Urbica *(wife of Carus)*	283–5	2
Numerian	282–4	12
Carinus	283–5	19
Diocletian	284–305	38
Maximian	286–305	22
Total, Central Empire		**14,788**

Gallic Empire	Dates	Total
Postumus	260–9	257
Laelian	269	4
Marius	269	35
Victorinus	269–71	7,494
Divus Victorinus	271	14
Tetricus I	271–4	12,416
Tetricus II	272–4	5,203
Gallic Empire, uncertain		2,954
Total, Gallic Empire		28,377
British Empire		
Carausius	286–93	766
Contemporary copies		314
Total, identifiable coins		44,245
Illegible coins		8,258
TOTAL		52,503

4.12 Above and right: Silver-washed radiate of Carinus (283–5), struck at Lyons (Frome Hoard) (23 mm)

4.13 Above and left: Copper alloy radiate of Maximian (286–305), struck at Ticinum (Pavia) (Frome Hoard) (23 mm)

CARAUSIUS

5.1 Below: Silver denarius of Carausius (286–93) (Frome Hoard) (also see fig. 5.12) (19 mm)

'In this outrageous act of brigandage [Carausius] first of all seized the fleet which had previously been protecting Gaul, and added a large number of ships which he built to the Roman pattern. He took over a legion [to Britain], intercepted some detachments of provincial troops, press-ganged Gallic tradesmen into service, lured over with spoils from the provinces numerous foreign forces, and trained them all under the direction of the ringleaders of this conspiracy for naval duties...' (Eumenius, Panegyric to Constantius Chlorus)

We are told that Carausius (fig. 5.1) was 'of very low birth', a Menapian who came from Holland or Belgium, and that he rose through the ranks of the Roman army, becoming a general under the emperor Maximian (286–305) (fig. 4.13). He apparently played a major role in bringing order back to Gaul after serious barbarian invasions and internal revolts. He was entrusted with command of the Roman fleet in the English Channel and North Sea so as to counter Saxon and Frankish raiders (fig. 5.2). We are told that he waited for the barbarians to sail away laden with booty before intercepting them; having taken back the loot, however, he did not return it to its rightful owners. This might just be a libellous story told by his enemies, but whatever the truth we know that he was sentenced to execution by Maximian and revolted.

Carausius was probably declared emperor at Rouen (Rotomagus) on the north French coast. A small, but significant number of coins in gold (fig. 5.3) and bronze were struck here at the start of his reign. He appears to have maintained control of northern France for most or all of his reign. However, his main base was to be Britain. One coin from the Frome Hoard shows Britannia receiving Carausius with a quotation taken from Virgil, 'come, long-awaited one' ('Expectate Veni') (fig. 5.4). Another coin shows his 'arrival' (Adventus), probably at London, which was to become his capital

5.2 Below: Copper alloy radiate of Allectus (293–6) showing a galley (19 mm) (BM CM1914,0411.31)

(fig. 5.5). In fact, most of our material evidence for Carausius comes from coins, there only being one other object that bears his name, a milestone found near Carlisle (fig. 5.6). The majority of Carausius' coins were struck in Britain, at London (fig. 5.8) and at another mint marked C or G (fig. 5.9). There has been debate for many years about where the 'C' mint was located – Colchester, Clausentum (Bitterne, near Southampton) and Glevum (Gloucester) have all been suggested – but the study of coin finds still does not present a clear answer.

Carausius undoubtedly had the support of the fleet and army of Britain; one of his coins declares his close ties to his military (fig. 5.10). It is highly likely that his forces made extensive use of the Saxon Shore Forts which had been constructed in the previous decade or so (fig. 5.7). The purpose of these forts is disputed, but they were probably built to house sailors and marines for the fleet, and also as bases to stockpile food and other items for export to the Continent. In the grounds of Dover Castle, way above the site

5.3 Opposite and above: Gold aureus of Carausius (286–93), probably struck in Rouen (Ashbourne Hoard; Derby Museum) (19/21 mm)

5.4 Above and left: Silver denarius of Carausius (286–93) showing Britannia greeting the emperor (Frome Hoard) (19 mm)

5.5 Above and left: Silver denarius of Carausius (286–93) showing the emperor riding (perhaps into London) (Frome Hoard) (19 mm)

5.6 Right: Roman milestone with the name of Carausius (286–93) found near Carlisle. After the reconquest of Britain, it was turned upside down and used for Constantine I (306–337) (Tullie House Museum, Carlisle)

5.7 Above: View of the interior of
Richborough Shore Fort, through the
postern gate (late third century AD)

of one such shore fort, you can still visit a lighthouse that was built in the third century (fig. 5.11).

Furthermore, Carausius was keen to promote himself as a *bona fide* Roman emperor – one of the coins from the Frome Hoard shows Romulus and Remus suckling the wolf (fig. 5.12), while he also celebrated consulships. Guy de la Bédoyère has convincingly argued that the letters RSR on the reverse of some Carausian coins stand for 'redeunt saturnia regna' (fig. 5.10). He also argues that the letters I.N.P.C.D.A., on a unique medallion of Carausius in the British Museum, probably mean 'iam nova progenies caelo demittitur alto' (fig. 5.13). These two inscriptions combine to provide two consecutive lines from Virgil's *Eclogues*, and translate as 'The Golden Age returns, now a new generation comes

5.11 Left:
The Roman
lighthouse at
Dover (3rd
century AD)

5.12 Right and above: Silver denarius of Carausius (286–93), showing Romulus and Remus suckling the wolf (Frome Hoard) (19 mm)

5.13 Above: Copper alloy medallion of Carausius (286–93) with the letters INCPDA (see page 28) (35mm) (BM CM1967,0901.1)

down from Heaven above.' Carausius is the only Roman emperor to quote classical Roman authors on his coins.

We know that Carausius was able to repel an invasion by the emperor Maximian in AD 288 or 289. In fact, this appears to be the first time that a British navy was used to defend our shores. After this Carausius felt confident enough to present himself as an equal partner with Diocletian and Maximian (fig. 5.14), although neither recognized him as such. However, Carausius was not able to defend himself against his finance minister, Allectus (fig. 5.2), who assassinated him in AD 293. We do not know the reason for the coup, but Allectus was able to rule in Britain for up to three years before the emperor Constantius Chlorus finally reconquered the island in AD 296 (fig. 5.15).

5.14 Left: Copper alloy coin struck by Carausius (286–93) showing (left to right) himself, Diocletian and Maximian ('C' Mint) (22 mm) (BM CM1977,0903.1)

5.15 Below left and below right: Gold medallion struck in Trier, showing Constantius and his fleet arriving at London in AD 296 (Arras Hoard, France; electrotype) (41 mm)

Not only do the five silver denarii and around 800 radiates found at Frome constitute the largest ever group of Carausian coins found, they also contain varieties never seen before, providing more evidence about the reign of Britain's 'forgotten emperor'.

CHAPTER

VI | OTHER COIN HOARDS FROM BRITAIN

6.1 Above: **A selection of coins from the Cunetio Hoard**

While the Frome Hoard is the largest hoard ever found in a single pottery container in Britain and the second largest hoard of any period, hoards of radiate coins buried between AD 253 and 296 are extremely common in Britain: nearly 600 hoards are known, a greater concentration than anywhere else in the Roman Empire.

Key:

■ Saxon Shore Fort
◇ Other late Roman Shore Fort
+ Important coin hoard
● Late Roman provincial capitals

Hadrian's Wall

◇ Maryport

◇ Lancaster

● York

+ Normanby

Caer
Gybi ◇

Ashbourne
+

Brancaster ■

Burgh ■

Elveden +

Walton ■

+ Chalgrove

Cardiff ◇

Bradwell ■

LONDON ●

+ Cunetio

Reculver ■

Richborough ■

+ Frome

Blackmoor
+

Dover ■

Lympne ■

Portchester ■

Pevensey ■

Some of these hoards are very large: the Cunetio Hoard (fig. 6.1), found near Marlborough in Wiltshire in 1978, had slightly more coins than Frome, 54,951, but it was found in two containers. The Cunetio Hoard closed with coins of Tetricus I (271–4) and was buried about twenty years earlier than Frome Hoard. Another huge hoard of this period, with 47,912 coins in a single pot, was found at Normanby in Lincolnshire in 1985. Like Frome, its latest coins were of Carausius – it had sixty nine coins from the earliest issues of his reign and so it may have been buried about five years before the Frome Hoard. The next largest hoard, found at Blackmoor in Hampshire in 1873, had 29,802 coins and closed with issues of Carausius' successor Allectus: its burial may be connected with Constantius's recovery of Britain in AD 296. Most hoards of this period are, however, much smaller, such as the Chalgrove Hoard which contained 4,957 coins, including only the second known coin of Domitian II (fig. 6.3).

As may be inferred from the large quantity of coins recovered from hoards, huge numbers of coins were being struck at this period. The radiate, which by about AD 270 was a coin of almost pure copper, was the only denomination being issued, apart from very limited issues of gold coins, and the Roman state issued it in great quantities. According to

6.3 Above and below: Copper alloy radiate of Domitan II (271), from the Chalgrove Hoard (Ashmolean Museum) (20 mm)

one estimate it is possible that under Victorinus and Tetricus the Gallic Empire was making around five to six million coins a week. This is production on a vast scale which was not equalled until the introduction of mechanical coin striking in the seventeenth and eighteenth centuries.

The high number of coin hoards of this period from Britain has long puzzled scholars. Traditionally it has been assumed that the hoards of coins and other valuables were buried by their owners because they were concerned about the threat of invasion (from raiders from Ireland on the western side of Britain or in the east from Saxons from Germany) and they buried their wealth in the ground with the intention of coming back in more peaceful times to recover it. An example of this is graphically described by Samuel Pepys in his diary: deeply worried by the Dutch raids on the Medway and Thames in June 1667, he took all the gold coins he could lay his hands on in London (£2,300 worth) and sent his wife and servant to bury them on the family estate in Brampton, Northamptonshire. In October, when the threat had past, he went back to retrieve them but had great difficulty finding where his wife had hidden the coins and, even after a great deal of digging, ended up £20–£30 short of the amount that had been buried.

Doubtless many hoards were buried in similar circumstances in Roman Britain and were recovered by their owners so that no trace of them survives today. On this model, we assume that the hoards found today are those which were not recovered by their owners – perhaps because they had been killed or because they had fled from Britain never to return. One problem with this picture is that the archaeological evidence shows that the late third century was generally a time

"According to one estimate it is possible that under Victorinus and Tetricus the Gallic Empire was making around five to six million coins a week."

of peace and prosperity in Britain. Although the populations in towns seem to have been declining, many villas were being built or expanded with luxurious new mosaics (fig. 8.1). There is little evidence for barbarian raids on the province in contrast, for example, to northern France at this time.

In fact the Frome Hoard calls the traditional interpretation of hoarding into question. If the original owners of this hoard had intended to come back and recover it later then surely they would have buried their coins in smaller containers that would have been easier to recover. The only way anyone could have recovered this hoard would have been by breaking the pot and scooping the coins out of it, which would have been awkward. We therefore suggest that it was most likely that the person or persons who buried this hoard put it in the ground without intending to come back and recover it. The hoard was found in an important agricultural area and it is possible that it was a sacrifice made to bring a good harvest, a successful breeding season or even clement weather (fig. 6.4).

One phenomenon which is highlighted by the sheer range of metal finds being recorded by the Portable Antiquities Scheme is how common the ritual burial or deposition of metal was in the Bronze and Iron Ages. Maybe this tradition continued in Britain into the Roman period with coin hoards? Britain has more coin hoards in proportion to its area than any other province in the Roman Empire. Was the Frome Hoard the possession of one person? Or was it the combined wealth of a wider community, each family or group contributing its share? This sort of question can only be answered by carrying out further work on the archaeological context of the findspot and by a thorough re-examination of coin hoards of this period.

"It was most likely that the person or persons who buried this hoard put it in the ground without intending to come back and recover it."

CHAPTER

VII | THE
SILIQUA
HOADR

7.1 Right: and below:Anonymous silver half-siliqua, mint of Trier, AD 375–92 (13 mm)

The intriguing possibility that the hoard may have been buried for ritual purposes, which is only a theory at present, is given a further twist by the fact that Dave Crisp had already found another hoard of Roman coins, consisting of sixty two silver siliquae of the fourth century (figs 7.1, 7.2, 7.3, 7.4), within a hundred metres of where the radiate hoard was found.

The siliquae were spread over an area of about 30 by 40 metres and were not associated with a container: this may have been a cloth or leather bag or purse which has not survived. These coins are undoubtedly from a hoard that had been scattered by ploughing: it would have been buried shortly after the date of the latest coin, which is of the emperor Eugenius, AD 392–4. After Mr Crisp's discovery a search on the Somerset Historic Environment Record revealed a hitherto little-known record of a hoard of 111 siliquae found during drainage works on a field on this same farm in 1867, and also a first-century Roman brooch, now in the Ashmolean Museum, Oxford. The relationship between the recently found coins and the 1867 hoard is not clear. There is no detailed record of the earlier find, but six coins,

of emperors from Julian II (AD 355–63) to Magnus Maximus (AD 383–8), are in the collection of Somerset County Council Heritage Service at Taunton: coins of all these emperors were also present in Mr Crisp's hoard. It is therefore highly likely that these two groups of coins came from the same hoard.

The coins are of the following emperors:

	Dates	Quantity
Constantius II	337–61	7
Julian II, as Caesar	355–60	1
Julian II, as Augustus	360–3	10
Jovian	363–4	2
Valentinian I	364–75	1
Valens	364–78	15
Gratian	367–83	10
Valentinian II	375–92	3
Theodosius I	379–95	3
Magnus Maximus	383–8	6
Arcadius	383–408	1
Eugenius	392–4	1
Anonymous half-siliqua	375–92	1
Uncertain emperor	364–78	1
Total		62

7.3 Above and top: Silver siliqua of Gratian, AD 367–83, mint of Trier (18 mm)

The discovery of two hoards, deposited about a hundred years apart, in close proximity to each other is unusual, but not unprecedented: four hoards of Roman coins of the third and fourth centuries AD are known to have been found in Shapwick, also in Somerset.

7.4 Left and above: Silver siliqua of Magnus Maximus, (383–8), mint of Trier. Maximus was declared emperor in Britain (17 mm)

CHAPTER

VIII | THE WIDER AREA

The town of Frome is situated in the north-east of Somerset, close to the border with Wiltshire. During the later third century the area around where the hoard was found would have been predominantly rural, with a dispersed population. The nearest towns were Shepton Mallet, 14 km to the west, and the much larger Bath, 23 km to the north.

8.1 Left: Dido and Aeneas in a panel from the Low Ham mosaic. The mosaic, found in an exceptionally large Somerset villa, depicts scenes from Virgil's tragic love story.

The population and economic role of larger towns such as Bath had begun to decline during this century and instead activity was beginning to shift to rural areas. By contrast, however, the smaller town of Shepton Mallet was at the height of its modest prosperity in the third and fourth centuries, with a number of stone buildings being constructed there at this time. This shift was also characterised by the development of greater numbers of often lavish aristocratic country villas. Indeed, evidence of a large villa or settlement site was discovered by archaeologists a few miles away from the site of the Frome Hoard and may well have been occupied during this period.

Although these villas would have provided a focus for economic activity, the majority of the population probably lived in smaller agricultural settlements and the remains of some of these have been discovered in the nearby area. We also know that a road ran fairly close by, joining and crossing the Fosse Way just north of Shepton Mallet before continuing west towards the lead mines around Charterhouse-on-Mendip. In its easterly direction the road ran on to Old Sarum, where it connected with routes to the coast, providing an important means of trade and communication. By comparison the evidence that we have about the immediate area surrounding the location of the Frome Hoard is fairly limited. The Somerset Historic Environment Record does not suggest any Roman activity on this particular site and a geophysical survey undertaken by GSB Prospection following the excavation of the hoard revealed little of significance. Dave Crisp has reported ninety other Roman finds from the locality, and Roman pottery from the same field. Undoubtedly more work needs to be done in the area.

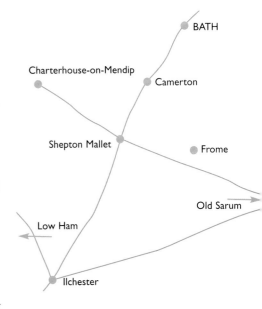

8.2 Above: Principal towns and road links of Somerset

CHAPTER

IX | WHAT HAPPENS NEXT?

The Frome Hoard and the siliqua hoard were both declared Treasure on 22 July 2010 by Mr Tony Williams, H M Coroner for East Somerset. Under the terms of the Treasure Act 1996 in law the hoards are the property of the Crown, but in practice they are offered to museums to acquire.

Somerset County Council Heritage Service expressed an interest in acquiring both finds intact at an early stage. The next step is for the hoards to be valued by the independent Treasure Valuation Committee to establish their full market value. The Committee, whose members are appointed by the Secretary of State for Culture, Media and Sport, will receive valuations from two experts and will give the finder, the landowner and the Heritage Service an opportunity to comment on these or to commission their own valuations. Once the valuation has been agreed by all parties, then the Heritage Service will have up to four months to raise the money needed, which will be shared equally by Dave Crisp and the landowner. Given the great public interest in the hoard we hope this campaign will be successful. All being well, Somerset Heritage Service hope to be able to display the hoards with the restored pot at the opening of the new Museum of Somerset in Taunton in 2011.

The project to conserve and study the hoard will progress alongside this. At present, 11,212 coins cannot be identified at all and the coins need to be fully cleaned before any detailed study can be undertaken. It will be a year's work for one conservator to clean the whole hoard and the British Museum is working with Somerset County Council Heritage Service to raise the necessary funds. Over the next couple of years, the authors hope to work on a full catalogue of the hoard and its interpretation, including a reassessment of the two other very large hoards from Cunetio and Normanby. There is no doubt that the Frome Hoard has many secrets still to reveal, both about itself and about its wider context.

Timeline

27 BC – AD 14	Reign of Augustus, first Roman emperor.
AD 43	Conquest of Britain by Claudius I.
60–61	Revolt of Boudica.
77–83	Governorship of Agricola, campaigns in Scotland.
122–8	Construction of Hadrian's Wall.
209–11	Septimius Severus campaigns in Scotland.
215	Introduction of a new denomination, the 'radiate' (sometimes known as the antoninianus) by Caracalla, tariffed at two denarii.
253	Accession of Valerian I who makes his son Gallienus co-emperor.
260	Capture of Valerian by Shapur I, Sasanian ruler; establishment of separate Gallic Empire by Postumus in Britain, Gaul and Spain. Gallienus remains ruler of the rump 'Central Empire'.
268	Assassination of Gallienus; succeeded by Claudius II as ruler of the Central Empire.
269	Assassination of Postumus after he suppressed the revolt of Laelian in Mainz; succeeded (briefly) by Marius and then by Victorinus. Central Empire regains control of Spain.
270	Claudius II dies of plague and is succeeded briefly by his brother Quintillus then by Aurelian.
271	Victorinus assassinated and succeeded by Tetricus I, formerly governor of Aquitania in south-west Gaul. Brief rebellion of Domitian II occurs at this time.
274	Aurelian defeats Tetricus I at Battle of Châlons-sur-Marne reuniting the Empire. Tetricus ends his days as governor of Lucania in southern Italy.
275	Aurelian assassinated and, after an interregnum, is succeeded by Tacitus.
276	Tacitus dies of fever or is assassinated and is succeeded briefly by his brother Florian, then by Probus.
282	Assassination of Probus, succeeded by Carus, who subsequently appoints his sons Numerian and Carinus co-rulers.
284	Diocletian proclaimed emperor by his troops and defeats Carinus.

285	Diocletian makes Maximian co-ruler and divides the Empire in two, taking the East, while Maximian has control of the West. Maximian starts issuing coins after being raised to the full rank of Augustus in 286.
286	Revolt of Carausius who establishes separate empire in Britain and part of northern Gaul.
288 or 289	Unsuccessful attempt by Maximian to reconquer Britain; Carausius subsequently starts striking 'coalition' coins in the names of Diocletian and Maximian.
293	Carausius assassinated by his finance minister Allectus. Loss of northern Gaul to Maximian.
296	Britain reconquered by Maximian's deputy Constantius I.

FURTHER READING

Abdy, Richard, *Romano-British Coin Hoards*, Shire Archaeology 82, 2002

Bédoyère, Guy de la, 'Carausius and the marks RSR and I.N.P.C.D.A.', *Numismatic Chronicle* 158 (1998), pp. 79–88

Besly, E.M. and Bland, R.F., *The Cunetio Treasure: Roman Coinage of the Third Century AD*, British Museum, 1983

Bland, R.F. and Burnett, A.M. (eds), *The Normanby hoard and other Roman Coin Hoards*, British Museum, 1988

Casey, P.J., *Carausius and Allectus: The British Usurpers*, Batsford, 1994

Ireland, S. (ed.), *Roman Britain: A Sourcebook*, 3rd edn, Routledge, 2008

Jackson, Ralph and Hobbs, Richard, *Roman Britain*, British Museum, 2010

Mann, J.C. and Penman, R.G., *Literary Sources for Roman Britain* (LACTOR 11, London Association for Classical Teachers, 2nd edition, 1985)

Mattingly, D., *An Imperial Possession. Britain in the Roman Empire 54 BC–AD 409*, Allen Lane, 2006

Reece, R., *The Coinage of Roman Britain*, Tempus, 2002

Robertson, Anne S. (edited by Hobbs, R. and Buttrey, T.V.) *Inventory of Romano-British Coin Hoards*, Royal Numismatic Society Special Publication 20, 2000

Salway, P., *Roman Britain, The Oxford History of England*, Oxford Paperbacks, 2001

PICTURE CREDITS